Usborne
Little First Stickers
Rainbows

Designed and illustrated by
Emily Beevers and Ian McNee
Additional artwork by Nick Wakeford

Words by Felicity Brooks

You'll find all
the stickers at the
back of the book.

Raindrops and rainbows

When raindrops plop onto petals, rainbow pixies and fairies come out to play. They splash in puddles, slide down toadstools and fly around the flowers. Can you add lots more to this scene?

SPLASH!

splish, splash

3

Rainbow painters

As the sun sparkles through the raindrops, it's time to make a rainbow appear in the sky. Stick on the fairies and pixies painting this enormous rainbow. Add some more unicorn helpers, too.

Rainbow Village

When the rainbow is ready, everyone flies home to Rainbow Village. Some relax on the rooftops, while others get busy with baskets, brooms and books. Can you finish this pretty picture?

Unicorn Meadow

Unicorn Meadow is a magical place full of happy unicorns and fantastic flowers. Stick on some unicorns flying over the rainbow, wading in the stream and watering the flowers.

Rainbow baking

Wonderful smells waft around the kitchen when the fairies and pixies bake cakes for a rainbow party. Fill the room with busy bakers and cover the tables with tasty rainbow treats.

Getting ready

It's time to get dressed for the rainbow party, and there are all kinds of shoes, clothes and hats to choose from. Stick on some more for the fairies and pixies to try on.

Sweet dreams

When the party is over, tired little fairies and pixies snuggle down in their rainbow beds and fall fast asleep. What do you think they could be dreaming about?

Rainbow painters pages 4-5

Sweet dreams page 16